Confirmation
The Spirit of Christ

by
Sr Mary David Totah OSB

All booklets are published thanks to the generous support of the members of the Catholic Truth Society

CATHOLIC TRUTH SOCIETY
PUBLISHERS TO THE HOLY SEE

CONTENTS

I went into retreat again for Confirmation, and I prepared myself with great care for the coming of the Holy Spirit; I can't understand how anyone could do otherwise before receiving this Sacrament of Love... Like the Apostles I waited for the promised Holy Spirit, and was overjoyed that soon I would be a perfect Christian, and have my forehead sealed eternally with the mystic cross of this great sacrament.

St Therese of Lisieux, The Story of a Soul

1. A Question-raising Sacrament

Dear Fr Murphy

I saw the notice in the parish bulletin about giving in your name for Confirmation next June, but I'm not sure yet whether the number of candidates from this family should be one, two or none! Our Karen is 14, the age you mention. She still goes to Mass on Sundays, and I know she prays. But when I suggested she get confirmed, she asked, 'Why?' and I didn't know what to say. All I can really remember about my own Confirmation is choosing a new name, trying to learn off by heart a list of fruits and gifts of the Spirit, and being tapped on the cheek by the bishop. It's not still like that, is it?

And after 20 years of marriage my husband has gradually started coming to Mass with me and the children. He was baptised as a baby, but brought up as nothing. I've told him that to join the Church properly, he's got to be confirmed - he says that confirmation is just for teenagers anyway! Yours sincerely, Julie Smith

Dear Mrs Smith,

Confirmation is not and never has been some form of puberty rite. Traditionally it belongs with baptism as part of the ceremony of Christian initiation. One of the reasons this sacrament is a little obscure is that it is difficult to disentangle it from baptism. In the East confirmation is given to infants immediately after their baptism. And it is now the policy of the Church that whenever adults, or children who reached the age of discretion, come to the church for baptism, they will normally be baptised, confirmed and make their First Holy Communion in a single liturgy. In the West, if someone has been baptised in infancy, his Confirmation is usually deferred for several years. As we'll see, this custom really grew up by accident rather than design.

Of course, if someone has been baptised as a baby, whether in the Catholic Church or in another denomination, but only comes to faith in Christ as an adult, he is not re-baptised, but he does need to be confirmed. Most parishes, including ours, run one programme of preparation for Confirmation for teenagers from Catholic families, and a separate programme for adults. Usually the teenagers are confirmed in a group during the bishop's visit. The adults, however, are usually "received into full communion with the Church" at the Easter Vigil, by being confirmed by the parish priest and making their First Holy Communion together with the adults who are being baptised then. The Easter Vigil is of course the climax of the year for the parish community, so it is the most appropriate time for a new member to be welcomed. If your husband is feeling very shy about his new faith, though, he could be received more quietly with only family and close friends present.

The light slap which used to be given on the cheek by the bishop is no longer the practice today. It was a sign of the blows we must be prepared to endure for Christ; as this booklet will explain, in this sacrament the Spirit brings a special strength of courage and perseverance in the face of difficulties and suffering. Your sincerely, Fr Murphy

Dear Fr Murphy,

All that is very reassuring and helpful; but what actually happens at Confirmation? Yours, Julie Smith

Dear Mrs Smith,

The rite of confirmation takes place in three main parts, which the body of this booklet will explain step-by-step. 1) The bishop, usually, together with the priests who may be associated with him, lay or extend hands over the candidates. 2) The celebrant says a prayer, going back to at least the early sixth century, asking the Father to send the Holy Spirit to be their helper and guide and give the sevenfold gift of wisdom and understanding, right judgment and courage, knowledge and reverence, wonder and awe. 3) the candidates are then signed on the forehead with chrism in the sign of the cross, saying, "N. Be sealed with the gift of the Holy Spirit". All the elements are meant to convey the giving of the Holy Spirit. Do let me know if you have any further queries. Yours, Fr Murphy

Dear Fr Murphy,

All that was most helpful. But I'm still not clear about the Holy Spirit. When the children were little I could tell them that God is a loving Father and the Jesus is their friend, but I didn't know what to say about the Holy Spirit, so I left him out. Yours sincerely, Julie Smith

Dear Mrs Smith,

Confirmation is often called the sacrament of the Spirit, or the seal of the Spirit. And because the Holy Spirit has somewhat dropped out of our horizon, it's no wonder that Confirmation has shared something of his fate! If Baptism primarily emphasises our union with Christ, in Confirmation the emphasis is more on our fellowship with the Holy Spirit. Confirmation completes the sacrament of Baptism.

There is, to be sure, a secret hidden quality about the Spirit, which makes it hard to speak or write about him.

This elusiveness is evident in the symbols used by Scripture to point towards him. He is like fire or water, or "a rushing, mighty wind" (*Acts* 2:2). Yet despite this mysterious quality about the Holy Spirit, the Church firmly states that the Spirit is a person, not just a hidden force like the "Force" in the *Star Wars* films; and so for all his seeming elusiveness, we can and do enter into personal relationship with him. For this to happen, Christ promised to send the Spirit. To become grown men and women in Christ, "perfect Christians," is to allow the Holy Spirit to live and act in us, to be guided by the Holy Spirit. What this means will vary from person to person. The important thing is to trust that God is transforming us, in his own way and in his own time, and to try as best we can to allow that to happen: to purify our hearts, to accept and deepen his gift, to put into practice what we carry in us, to grow in insight. The Spirit is what fills us, and incites us to seek God; he awakens our longing for God; the Spirit also awakens the desire for prayer in us; and the Spirit leads individuals to perceive where their call lies, the task God has given each one, and he gives us the power to fulfill that task. Yours, Fr Murphy

Dear Fr Murphy,

I find this a bit confusing. Don't we receive the Holy Spirit at Baptism? If so, then what is the point of Confirmation? Yours, Julie Smith

Dear Mrs Smith,

Yes, to be baptised in the name of Jesus is to be baptised in his Spirit (*1 Cor* 6:11; 12:13); it is to be reborn as children of God by water and the Spirit (*John* 3:5ff; *1 John* 3:24). The Holy Spirit comes to the baptised and gives them his gifts. But, there is a *further coming* of the Spirit in Confirmation and a special increase in his gifts for the growth and increase of our spiritual life, and for a life of Christian witness. The giving of the Spirit is never completed, because the life of God is inexhaustible and infinite. That's why the Spirit is active in all the sacraments, with different signs and for different purposes, even if the final object of every coming of the Spirit is always communion with God.
Yours, Fr Murphy

Dear Fr Murphy,

One last question: did Jesus institute this sacrament? I can't find it in the Bible. Thank you for all your trouble.
Yours, Julie Smith

Dear Mrs Smith,

This has been up for debate. Some said confirmation was instituted by the apostles; while others have pointed to places in the New Testament where Christ may have instituted the sacrament, as when he breathed on the apostles, and said, "Receive the Holy Spirit" (*John* 20:22).

Thomas Aquinas said that Christ instituted the sacrament of confirmation not by demonstrating it but by *promising* it. "I shall ask the Father, and he will give you another Advocate to be with you forever, the Spirit of truth...(*Jn* 14:17) "It is better for you that I go; if I fail to go the Paraclete will never come to you" (*Jn* 16:17). Christ had promised his apostles to send the Holy Spirit.

Here we are at the very heart of the meaning of Confirmation, so forgive me if I go on a bit!

For Luke this promise was fulfilled on the day of Pentecost. Jesus told his disciples after his resurrection not to leave Jerusalem but to await their baptism with the Holy Spirit, promising them:

> You shall receive power when the Holy Spirit has come upon you; and you shall be my witnesses in Jerusalem and in all Judea and Samaria and to the ends of the earth (*Acts* 1:4-8).

On the feast of Pentecost the Spirit erupts among the apostles in tongues of flame and thunder, flooding weak men with new courage and joy. They receive power to bear witness in their words and in their lives to Christ. Peter explains this as the fulfillment of an Old Testament prophecy: "And in the last days, it shall be, God declares, that I shall pour out my Spirit upon all flesh" (*Joel* 2:28-32; *Acts* 2:16-21).

We may never know precisely what happened on the day of Pentecost, but we do know that it was one of the supremely great days in the Church's life. From that moment on, the Holy Spirit became the dominant reality in the life of the early Church. The effect of the Spirit on the first community was immediate and striking. They were indeed filled with "power from on high" (*Luke* 24.49). And the rest of the book of Acts is a testimony to the presence and work of the Spirit in the primitive Church. We see individuals transformed, moved to faith, love, prayer, to a life often in contradiction to an unbelieving world. The Spirit sends Paul off on his missionary journeys, guides him explicitly at each turning point; the Spirit inspires the leaders of the Church when important decisions are to be made. The Spirit is the source of day-to-day courage and power, giving Christians the strength to meet dangerous situations, the eloquence they need, and joy in the midst of everything. All this is shown to be life in the Spirit.

But the gift of the Spirit was not confined to those present on the day of the first Pentecost. As Peter explained, what had happened on that day was a realisation of the prophecies from the Old Testament that the Spirit would be poured out on *all* people... In his sermon immediately following the event, Peter said, "This is what was foretold by the prophet Joel" (*Acts* 2:16-18). Peter went on to describe how others were to receive it:

> Repent and be baptised, every one of you, in the name of Jesus Christ, to have your sins forgiven; then you will receive the gift of the Holy Spirit. This promise is for you and your children, and for all those however far away, whom the Lord calls to himself (*Acts* 2:37).

Note how Baptism is the first requirement; the gift of the Spirit follows upon it.

Such was the realisation of Pentecost; such was the promise of the Father; such is the grace of Confirmation for each one of us, the sign that the fullness of the Holy Spirit is given to the whole people of God. Yours, Fr Murphy

2. THE EFFECTS OF CONFIRMATION

Unites us more firmly to Christ

Baptism is equivalent to birth; we are born of God, made sons and daughters of the Father in Christ Jesus. The complete renewal of our nature with the bestowal of the Spirit are given in baptism, in germ as it were. But the gift has to unfold and reveal all it contains gradually. The help of the Spirit is required here too, for growth in Christian life. Baptism gives us this treasure, Confirmation, or rather the Holy Spirit, is the key that unlocks it. All is given in baptism; confirmation confirms, establishes, makes its deeper, firmer, extending it to the whole of our life. We live in time; God wills us to co-operate at each succeeding moment to bring about the full flowering of the initial gift.

"Baptism gives us this treasure, Confirmation is the key that unlocks it"

By baptism we enter into God's family, we pass from death to life; we become *living ones,* alive in Christ; in Confirmation we are *life-giving.* If baptism makes us sons and daughters of the Father in Christ Jesus, Confirmation makes us witnesses and transmitters of this new life within us. By baptism we have put on Christ, been *clothed with Christ* that he may live in us; in Confirmation we are made capable of *spreading Christ.*

By Baptism we are *called* and justified, in order to be glorified (*Rom* 8:29). By Confirmation we are *sent* to make disciples of all nations (*Mt* 28:19); to this end we are clothed with power from on high (*Lk* 24:29).

By baptism we become *disciples,* among those who heart the word and put it into practice; in Confirmation, we become *prophets,* possessing the power to witness to Christ and bring truth to one's neighbour.

Like Baptism, Confirmation confers a ***character;*** as an act of Christ and of his Church it cannot be repeated. St Thomas Aquinas said that the character of baptism enabled the Christian to do whatever pertains to his own salvation. In the character of Confirmation, Christians receive the power to attain spiritual perfection and fight temptation. "In this sacrament the Holy Sprit is given for strength; just as he was given to the Apostles on the day of Pentecost ...the grace bestowed in this sacrament does not differ from that bestowed in Baptism but increases what is already there."

By the character, we are marked, as it were, by the ceremony and remain forever someone who has been

Go, therefore, make disciples of all the nations; baptise them in the name of the Father and of the Son and of the Holy Spirit, (Matt 28:19)

confirmed. The character means we are marked, branded, we are possessed by God, or rather, disposed to being possessed. It is power, a talent for being a Christian that has to be developed. It is like the outline of a drawing, crying out to be coloured in. It brings with it a great capacity - for worship, prayer, the reception of the other sacraments. Or to use another analogy, it is like a muscle that wants to be used. In Baptism and Confirmation we have a muscle for living the Christian life. From this point of view there is no objection to giving the sacraments to infants and young children, for they will have within themselves the principle enabling them to act as witnesses of Christ when they develop.

This character is indelible; it cannot be effaced. That is why if someone is confirmed as a child or teenager, but later gives up his faith, he is still in potential a full member of the Church. He is like the prodigal son who left home without appreciating what a wonderful place it was to be. If later on he decides to return, the Church will welcome him back with the joy of the prodigal son's father: "Let us eat and make merry, for this my son was dead and is alive again" (*Lk* 15:23-24). The *effects* of the sacrament - boldness in confessing Christ, strength, responsibility for mission - may be blocked by our sin or unbelief, but given our collaboration, the character is a guarantee of that sacramental grace's abiding power.

Makes us "perfect" Christians

"After the font it remains for the perfecting to take place." St Ambrose

Up until the ninth century the rite of confirmation was frequently called the rite of "perfection," completion or sealing. Confirmation has much the same meaning as when we refer to a business affair being signed and sealed: completed, finished, ratified.

Confirmation is a perfecting or completing of the work begun in baptism. It confers grace beyond that already received and imparts a new sacramental character. But this completing or perfecting of Baptism must be carefully understood. Baptism is complete and perfect in itself; nothing is lacking in it in terms of grace and salvation. The perfection of confirmation is a perfection of superabundance. Note how *The Catechism of the Catholic Church* uses comparatives when speaking of the grace of confirmation: "it roots us *more* deeply in the divine filiation...; it unites us *more* firmly to Christ; it increases the gifts of the Spirit in us; it renders our bond with the church *more* perfect" (1303) [emphasis added]. Confirmation brings the superabundance of Pentecost.

> it roots us more deeply in the divine filiation...; it unites us more firmly to Christ; it increases the gifts of the Spirit in us; it renders our bond with the church more perfect (CCC 1303)

It is a question of becoming more perfectly what we are already: children of God. The anointing at Confirmation seals, makes safe, establishes the candidate in the Holy Spirit and, as the prayer for the Spirit over the candidates indicates, "completes" the process of initiation in which the Spirit has been active all along. That's why it is said that Confirmation makes us "perfect Christians"; it brings a "perfecting grace" that establishes a person fully in the Church, with all the responsibilities and privileges that entails. The word perfect can be misleading. In its primary sense it means completing, accomplishing, achieving something that has been begun. It is not primarily a perfecting of the candidate in the moral or psychological order, although, as in baptism and the Eucharist this is on the horizon.

The Eucharist perfects Confirmation

If Confirmation perfects what has been bestowed in Baptism, both Baptism and Confirmation are completed in the Eucharist. Confirmation's connection with the Eucharist is important. The Eucharist is the perfecting of both Baptism and Confirmation. These three sacraments form the Church's rite of initiation. As Aidan Kavanagh has remarked, "The most immediate vocation of the baptised and confirmed is to stand before God in worship at the Table."[1] Baptism and

[1] *Confirmation: Origins and Reform* (New York: Pueblo, 1988), p. 87.

Confirmation prepare us for the Eucharist, and the Eucharist renews the grace of both. By celebrating the Eucharist we enter more fully into the mystery of Christ's death and resurrection which we began to share at baptism; it also renews the anointing of Confirmation, which is the personal Pentecost of each Christian. At each Mass we invoke the Holy Spirit, not only upon the gifts but also upon the people who receive them, renewing that full gift of the Spirit they received at Confirmation. The dismissal at Mass is also an echo of our sending forth at Confirmation to become messengers of Christ and heralds of the Gospel.

Increases the gifts of the Holy Spirit in us

St Thomas Aquinas described Confirmation as "the fullness of the Holy Spirit."[2] According to the Catechism, the main effect of the sacrament of Confirmation is "the special outpouring of the Holy Spirit as once granted to the Apostles on the day of Pentecost." To be a complete Christian means the Holy Spirit guiding my life through his gifts. The Holy Spirit's personal name is Gift; he is the source of all gifts. "Come giver of gifts" we say in our Pentecost liturgy. The Spirit comes to give us gifts that have to be used.

When we think of the gift of the Spirit we might be tempted to think of gifts and graces that are unexpected,

---

[2] *Ibid.*, a.6.

dramatic, spectacular - like the gift of tongues (where someone is given to speak about God in words he doesn't understand), or healing or miracle-working. St Paul does mention these. But he also speaks of the variety of functions in the Church as gifts: first apostles, second prophets, third teachers, helpers administrators - all those things that build up the church. As well as these institutional gifts there are the gifts of the Spirit: the spirit of wisdom and understanding, the spirit of counsel and fortitude, the spirit of knowledge and piety, the spirit of the fear of the Lord. These gifts are already found in the prophet Isaiah (11:2).

"The seven gifts are really one: areas of activity in which the Spirit will make his presence felt"

The prayer before Confirmation speaks of this sevenfold Gift with which the candidate will be endowed. The sevenfold gift also points to the way the Holy Spirit is ever ready to serve and help us. (That is why we speak of the Spirit as the "Paraclete," which is a Greek word for someone who comes to another's help, an advocate.) He helps us and serves us by giving us insight and understanding of the things of God, by giving us the strength for resolute and courageous witness, a strength that comes with abandoning ourselves to the strength of God; by filling us with a tender love and devotion for God. The seven gifts are really one: areas of activity in which the Spirit will make his presence felt. As well as these seven gifts, St Paul speaks of the fruits of the Spirit: Love, joy, peace, patience, kindness and goodness, faithfulness, gentleness, self-control. All this is what it is to live a life in the Spirit, to be a confirmed Christian. We will see the Spirit working in us when we see his fruits. To be a confirmed Christian is to use the gifts you are given for the good of all. Each believer has the right and duty to use these gifts in the Church and in the world. These gifts are to be sought and prayed for

Although we have become accustomed to speak of the seven gifts of the Spirit, the liturgy means the one gift, the gift of the Spirit himself. In Confirmation we are given a particular grace to be open to the work of the Spirit, in the same way as Christ, Our Lady, and the Apostles opened themselves to the prompting of the Spirit and performed their work in the Spirit. The sacrament of Confirmation is the sacrament of the mysterious influence of the Spirit upon the whole life of each Christian.

Perfects our bond with the Church

Through Confirmation the baptised are "more perfectly bound to the Church".[3] The grace of Confirmation should awaken "the sense of belonging to the Church."[4] Through Baptism and Confirmation we are enabled to

[3] *The Catechism of the Catholic Church* 1285; hereafter *CCC*.
[4] *CCC* 1309

make and become a self-gift to the Church for the good of the Church, and through her, for the whole world. The result is what tradition has called the *anima ecclesiastica,* the soul conformed to the Church, a soul which goes beyond its narrowness to embrace the dimensions of the mission of Christ and of the Church. The confirmed Christian grows in his consciousness of thinking with the Church and in the Church, of identifying himself or herself with the Church's intentions.

This ecclesial dimension of Confirmation is important for any understanding of the sacrament. It is underscored by this sacrament's close association with the bishop, whether by allowing only the bishop to confirm, as has been the Roman practice, or by insisting that only chrism consecrated by the bishop could be used, as in the East. Just as the apostles after Pentecost imparted the Spirit by the laying on of hands, so the bishop does through Confirmation. This practice "more clearly expresses the communion of the new Christian with the bishop as guarantor and servant of the unity, catholicity, and apostolicity of his church, and hence the connection with

This practice more clearly expresses the communion of the new Christian with the bishop as guarantor and servant of the unity, catholicity, and apostolicity of his church, and hence the connection with the apostolic origins of Christ s Church (CCC 1292)

the apostolic origins of Christ's Church" (*CCC* 1292). Confirmation thus strengthens one's bond with the bishop. The bishop is so closely involved because he is the successor of the Apostles who received the Spirit at Pentecost and the power to transmit the Spirit through the laying on of hands; and because he embodies in his own person the local church, and the wider Church. As far back as the second century, St Ignatius of Antioch expressed this conviction powerfully and succinctly: "Wherever the bishop is, there let the people be, just as wherever Christ Jesus is, there is the Catholic Church."

Although the bishop is the "original" and "normal" minister of confirmation, if the need arises, the bishop may grant the faculty of administering confirmation to a priest; priests may also confirm under extraordinary circumstances, as in missionary territories or in danger of death. Priests who baptise an adult or a child not baptised in infancy, or admit a baptised person into full communion with the church may also confirm, as these will receive Baptism, Confirmation and the Eucharist in one service.

Strength to be true witnesses of Christ

Baptism incorporates the individual into the Church which is the Body of Christ; Confirmation brings with it a new factor, what the Catechism calls the "stricter obligation" of the confirmed "to spread the faith by word and by deed," to proclaim by a whole way of life the salvation won for the world by Jesus Christ. The rite of Confirmation gives evidence of this in still another way. The laying on of hands found in the rite represents not only the outpouring of the Spirit; from the earliest days of the Church it has also been the sign of being established in ministry, of being sent on mission: "You will receive power from the Holy Spirit who will descend upon you. You will thus be my witnesses in Jerusalem, in all of Judea and Samaria, and unto the ends of the earth" (*Acts* 1:8). The same promise of Pentecost belongs as well to all those who are confirmed.

"Mission consists in making Christ present to the world through personal witness"

The work of the Spirit is to form us into another Christ who was sent out on mission from his Father. This does not mean all will be called to the missionary field; nor is it an invitation for all of us to change our jobs. To be an apostle, a witness, means to have a life, not a job. The first characteristic of apostolic life is sharing of the life of the Lord: Jesus summoned the apostles "to be with him" and to be sent out to preach (*Mk* 3:14). Being with Jesus comes first and is the first mark of the apostle. They were called by him just to be with him; the fundamental law of any apostolate is union with Christ. Indeed, more than in external works, mission consists in making Christ present to the world through personal witness. This is the challenge, this is the primary task of the confirmed.

The more Christians allow themselves to be conformed to Christ, the more Christ is made present and active in the world for the salvation of all. Christians are 'in mission' by virtue of their very consecration in Baptism and Confirmation; and they bear witness in accordance with their vocation in life. Like the Spirit himself, the confirmed Christian is at work everywhere, wherever he finds himself. St Paul himself was profoundly convinced of the fruitfulness not only of his work but also of his sufferings for the Church as a whole. [Indeed the most important acts exchanged in this communion are praying for others and suffering for others, since they are most closely linked to Christ's own being and acting for others.] These things are at least as important as the external, visible mutual help and witness that is a matter of course for Christians.

> The real apostolate, consists precisely in participation in the salvific work of Christ. Christ redeemed the world, a slave to sin, principally by prayer and the sacrifice of himself. In like manner, souls that strive to re-live this intimate aspect of the mission of Christ, even if they do not give themselves to any external activity, really contribute to the apostolate in an eminent manner (Pope John XXIII)[5]

---

[5] *Allocution to Cistercian Abbots,* Rome, September 1962

Confirmation commits us to preaching, in one way or another, directly or indirectly, the mighty works of God.

If at Confirmation we are given strength from on high to become witnesses of Christ, joy is one of the secrets of that strength. Those confirmed are anointed with the "oil of gladness." Pope John Paul wrote an encyclical about evangelisation called *Redemptoris Missio,* and his final words in it point to the importance of joy in spreading the Gospel: "The characteristic of every authentic missionary life is the inner joy that comes from faith. In a world tormented and oppressed by so many problems, a world tempted to pessimism, the one who proclaims the 'Good News' must be a person who has found true hope in Christ." Joy is given for witness.

Strength to defend the faith

"Reborn in baptism for life... confirmed after baptism for the strife" (Faustus of Riez, 5th C)

At his baptism, Our Lord was anointed by the Spirit for his work of proclaiming the good news. Immediately afterwards we find the Spirit leading him into the

The characteristic of every authentic missionary life is the inner joy that comes from faith. In a world tormented and oppressed by so many problems, a world tempted to pessimism, the one who proclaims the Good News must be a person who has found true hope in Christ.

wilderness to do battle with the devil, whose work he was to destroy by miracles and healing, and ultimately by his death and resurrection. At Pentecost itself there was such a strengthening; the first Christians became witnesses of Christ, spokesmen for his cause. Before Pentecost an Apostle could deny Christ; after it they were martyrs. Martyr is the Greek word for witness. To bear witness to Christ is to encounter opposition, persecution, and often death. Included in the gift of Pentecost was the call to martyrdom. The light slap which used to be given on the cheek by the bishop after the anointing was a sign of the blows we must be prepared to endure for Christ. And the oil of the anointing recalls the anointing of athletes and wrestlers, with all its associated ideas of defence and strengthening. Confirmation shows martyrdom to be a universal vocation.

There is a constant tradition attributing to Confirmation the grace of strength, especially for bearing witness even unto martyrdom, and for spiritual combat. In the fifth century St Cyril of Jerusalem exhorted his catechumens:

> Just as Christ after his baptism and visitation by the Holy Spirit went out and successfully wrestled with the enemy, so you also, after your holy baptism and sacramental anointing, put on the armour of the Holy Spirit, confront the power of the enemy, and reduce it saying: 'I can do all things in Christ who strengthens me.'

Confirmation makes us Christian soldiers. "This sacrament is given to man for strength in spiritual combat," noted St Thomas Aquinas. "Though he who is baptised is made a member of the Church, nevertheless he is not yet enrolled as a Christian soldier."[6] This is about something much more than the personal struggle of adolescents with which this sacrament is frequently associated; it concerns the ongoing struggle between the mystery of salvation and the mystery of iniquity (2 *Thess* 2:7) which constitutes the secret history of the whole of humanity. Confirmation invites us to take seriously the realities of spiritual combat against the forces of evil in our time, against what the Holy Father has called "the culture of death." It is a question of entering into the combat of Christ, with Christ. We have a powerful expression of the reality of spiritual combat in *The Lord of the Rings,* where it is seen that the one power before which evil is helpless is sacrifice, self-offering. Frodo, Gandalf and Aragorn are all in their different ways martyrs, Christ-figures who undergo different kinds of voluntary deaths and resurrections. In this kind of battle, strength is overcome by weakness, pride and power by humility, tyranny by martyrdom. In this world and the world of the Gospel, the self is only saved when it is lost, found only when given away in

[6] *Summa,* q.72, a. 9.

sacrifice. Sacrifice, humility, love, fidelity - these are shown to be the strongest, and most overlooked, weapons against evil. We can recall too St Maximilian Kolbe voluntarily taking the place of another prisoner and going instead to die in his place.

"The true Christian will be a constant martyr"

Christians today have particular reason to reflect on the centrality of martyrdom, for the century that has just come to a close has been pre-eminently an age of martyrs. In the 20 years between the two World Wars more Christians died for the faith than in the whole 300 years after the crucifixion. Not all of us will be called to die outwardly for Christ in the gas chamber or prison camps; that depends on circumstances beyond our control. What we can do, however, is to be prepared to carry our cross inwardly. Clement of Alexandria affirmed that the true Christian will be a constant martyr: "He will be a martyr by night and a martyr by day, a martyr in his speech, his daily life, his character."[7] Confirmation is a call to life-long self-offering, not one of great self-sacrifices but a multitude of small ones: in the mutual love in marriage and family life, in acts of personal and community service, in loyalty to the teachings of the Church's magisterium and in defence of the faith.

---

[7] Miscellanies 2:20.

What is essential in this is our fidelity to our Christian vocation. In both Baptism, particularly in the rite of renouncing Satan, and in Confirmation the Christian throws down a challenge to the forces of evil. This gives a meaning of love and redemption to the battles of everyday life.

3. THE LITURGY OF CONFIRMATION

Like all the other sacraments, confirmation is normally to be celebrated within the Mass, after the liturgy of the word.

> The whole people of God, represented by families and friends of the candidates and by members of the local communities will be invited to take part in the celebration and will express its faith in the fruits of the Holy Spirit. [8]

The place of the sacraments in Christian life needs to be seen in the context of a community of believers. They are celebrations of the Church, whereby she acknowledges her faith and commits herself to it. Non-Catholic relations and friends, and especially a non-Catholic parent, should be warmly welcomed. Even if they have different religious beliefs, their loving support and their example of a life of integrity will continue to be of great value to the Confirmation candidate, especially if he is still growing up.

Liturgy of the Word

The Scripture readings provided for the rite serve as an excellent starting point for showing the work of

---

[8] *RC*, 4

the Spirit in the Church and in Christian life. The first five texts are taken from the Old Testament and speak of the Anointed One who was to come to bring good news to the poor (*Isaiah* 11:1-4; *Isaiah* 42:1-3; *Isaiah* 61:1-3a, 6a, 8b-9); and the promise of a special pouring out of the Spirit within our hearts (*Ezekiel* 36:24-28) and on all mankind (*Joel* 2:23a, 26-30a). The readings from Acts show the Spirit poured out on the Church; the role of the Spirit in unifying and sustaining the Church is the special emphasis of 1 Cor 12:4-13 and Eph 4:1-6; whereas the other texts from St Paul speak of the transforming power of the Spirit in the lives of individuals: the Spirit as the gift of God's love (*Romans* 5:1-2, 5-8)), as bearing witness to our identity as children of God (*Romans* 8:14-17). The Spirit sets us free, teaches us how to pray, and enables us to lead lives characterised by joy, peace, love, patience, self-control, gentleness, fidelity - the "fruits of the Spirit" (*Romans* 8:26-27; *Galatians* 5:16-17, 22-25). The gospel readings on the baptism of Jesus (*Mark* 1:9-11) and at the beginning of his public ministry (*Luke* 4:16-22) show Jesus as the Servant of God, anointed by the Spirit of God for the work of salvation. It is this same Spirit that makes it possible for us to live the Gospel in the spirit of the beatitudes (*Matthew* 25:14-30; *Luke* 8:4-15; *Matthew* 5:1-12).

Presentation of the Candidates

The candidates are presented to the bishop by the parish priest or catechists. If they are children, they are to be presented by their parents or sponsors. To highlight the close union of Baptism and Confirmation, the Confirmation sponsor should ideally be the same person who stood for the Candidate at Baptism (*CCC* 1131). The sponsor must not only present the recipient to the bishop and guarantee his dispositions, but must also help and guide him in the struggles. Like the sponsor for baptism, the sponsor for Confirmation must always consider himself responsible for the godchild and see to his Christian upbringing and prepare him for Christian discipleship in the Church.

Unless they are very numerous the candidates are to be called by name. It is sometimes customary to choose another patron saint for one's confirmation. In this as in so much else, Confirmation echoes the naming ceremony in baptism. In Baptism the naming of the child is bound up with how he or she is identified before God (so that it is rightly called one's baptismal or Christian name; in Confirmation the choice of another name or patron saint has the added dimension of a commissioning-for-service. In the Bible God often gives a new name to those he enlists to collaborate with him in his work of salvation: Abram became Abraham, "the father of many nations, " and Simon became Peter, "the rock."

Renewal of Baptismal Promises

After the homily there is the *profession of faith.* The bishop says: "Before you receive the Spirit, be mindful of the faith which you or your parents or godparents professed with the church." If they were baptised as infants, this will be the first time that the candidates have made a public profession of faith. The formula makes clear that this is not a statement of personal opinion, but a statement of their faith in the saving power of God the Creator of heaven and earth, in the life, death and resurrection of Jesus Christ. Special mention is made of the Holy Spirit:

> Do you believe in the holy Spirit, the Lord, the giver of life, who came upon the apostles at Pentecost and today is given to you sacramentally in confirmation?
> **I do.**

The very same Spirit of God who was poured out on the Church at Pentecost remains with the Church today. It is this Spirit who will speak through us to the Church and to the world, each in one's own unique, irreplaceable way, but all for the same end: the building up of the Church.

If baptism expresses the death and resurrection of Christ, Confirmation has this special reference to Pentecost. Good Friday and Easter are to Pentecost what Baptism is to Confirmation. This connection has been made from the earliest times.[9] In the words of Pope Paul VI, Confirmation is the "perpetuation of Pentecostal grace in the Church."[10] The Baptism of the Christian is his Easter, while Confirmation renews for him the gift of Pentecost.

As in the life of Christ there were two stages to his paschal mystery - Easter and Pentecost - so in the life of the Church which is modelled on Christ's life - there are two stages for initiation into Christian life - Baptism and Confirmation. Just as the sending of the Holy Spirit at Pentecost put a "seal" on the paschal mystery, so Confirmation puts a seal on the baptised person. This means that our incorporation into the Church and our sacramental communion in the mysteries of Easter and Pentecost is perfected in two stages. Hence the two sacraments are clearly distinct (though always to be related) in the same way as the two mysteries which they represent sacramentally. But together they form the sacramental re-presentation of the one redeeming mystery of Christ, perfected to the full.

---

[9] Cf. St Augustine, *On the first Epistle of John* 6,10 in Turner, p.14-25. This is the guiding principle of St Thomas' treatment of Confirmation in the Summa, Cf. III, q.72, a.7. In 1439 the Council of Florence declared: "The effect of this sacrament consists in this: that the Holy Spirit is given for the strengthening of the Christian, just as he was given to the Apostles on the day of Pentecost, that the Christian may boldly profess the name of Christ."

[10] Apostolic Constitution on the Sacrament of Confirmation *Divinae consortium naturae* (1971)

The laying on of hands

After concluding the profession of faith, the bishop stands with his priests and says:

> Let us pray to our Father that he will pour out the Holy Spirit to strengthen his sons and daughters with his gifts and anoint them to be more like Christ the Son of God.

The ultimate goal of the Spirit is to transform us into the image of the Son.

After a period of silent prayer, the bishop and priests stretch out their hands over those to be confirmed. This ancient gesture is used in different ways in different sacramental liturgies - to invoke the Holy Spirit upon the gifts during Mass, to give a solemn blessing to the congregation at the end of Mass, to ordain a priest, to bless a newly married couple, to absolve the repentant sinner in Confession. In Confirmation it has always been associated with calling down the Holy Spirit and his gifts on the newly baptised. By the imposition of hands the gift of the Spirit is invoked, and by the anointing the gift is sealed.

Like that of anointing, the rite of the imposition of hands has roots that go back to the most ancient religious traditions of Israel (*Num* 8:10; 27:18; *Deut* 34:9). The imposition of hands is a gesture of blessing, consecration, investiture. It was the gesture used by Our Lord to bless children and heal the sick (*Mk* 6:5; *Lk* 13:13). The Apostles lay their hands on the seven deacons (*Acts* 6:6), Paul and Barnabas were sent on mission through the laying on of hands (*Acts* 13:3), and Paul reminds Timothy of that moment in 1Tim 4:14; 2 Tim 1:6.

The anointing with chrism

Every sacrament consists of some significant gesture or sign; this is known as the *matter* of the sacrament. Then there are words which make the symbolism explicit. These are known as the *form*. For Confirmation, what is the essential sign: imposition of hands or anointing? This question had exercised the minds of theologians for centuries; while in the West both the laying on of hands and anointing with chrism were employed, in the East only anointing was used. In his reform of the rite Pope Paul VI clarified any doubt concerning the future understanding of the rite when he decreed: "The sacrament of Confirmation is conferred through the anointing with chrism on the forehead, which is done by the laying on of hands, and through the words: Be sealed with the gift of the Holy Spirit."[11] The sign, or matter, of

Scholastic theologians analysed sacraments in terms of matter and form . The matter is the visible element or symbolic gesture, such as anointing with oil. The form is the actual words or prayer used, which brings out the significance of and makes explicit what is already there.

[11] Pope Paul VI, *Divinae consortium naturae,* (1971).

the sacrament is the *anointing with the holy oil,* called chrism. The new order sees the signing of the forehead *as* the imposition of the hand.

In using oil for her liturgy, the Church was continuing a practice of the Old Testament. The Hebrews poured out oil on holy stones and other objects, and anointed kings, priests and prophets with it. The meaning given to an anointing with sacred oil was the bestowal of holiness. The person or thing anointed was sanctified by Yahweh, the Holy One. Anointing too was closely associated with the giving of the Spirit. When Samuel anointed David as king the Spirit of God came upon him: "Then Samuel took the horn of oil and anointed him in the midst of his brothers, and the Spirit of the Lord came mightily upon David from that day forward" (*1 Sam* 16:13). Jesus takes on the Old Testament offices of priest, prophet and king when he is anointed by the Holy Spirit at his baptism. At the Jordan, with the outpouring of the Spirit, Jesus is manifested as "the Christ," which literally means "the anointed one". In Confirmation our baptismal anointing is confirmed and strengthened, and we become "another Christ" in Cyril of Jerusalem's words: "Now that you are reckoned worthy of this holy chrism, you are called Christians, and this title you substantiate by your new birth."

We are Christians because we are literally "anointed ones". The Catechism sums this up well: "The post-baptismal anointing with sacred chrism in Confirmation and ordination is the sign of consecration. By Confirmation Christians, that is those who are anointed, share more completely in the mission of Jesus Christ and the fullness of the Holy Spirit with which he is filled, so that their lives may give off 'the aroma of Christ.' (*2 Cor* 2:15)" (*CCC* 1294).

The oil used at Confirmation is consecrated by the bishop at the Chrism Mass during Holy Week. The Catechism (*CCC* 1297) sees the ceremony of the consecration of the chrism to be a sort of preparation liturgy of Confirmation. A prayer when the chrism is consecrated speaks of the "sanctifying power of anointing." The oil and the anointing reveal to the candidate and the assembled faithful that this new life is to be a holy life, guaranteed by the Spirit who is not only a Holy Spirit but a Spirit who *makes* holy, a sanctifying spirit. As Jesus is "sealed" as Christ by the Holy Spirit at his baptism, so too the believer at Confirmation becomes another Christ, sealed by the Spirit.

The post-baptismal anointing with sacred chrism in Confirmation and Ordination is the sign of consecration. By Confirmation Christians, that is those who are anointed, share more completely in the mission of Jesus Christ and the fullness of the Holy Spirit with which he is filled, so that their lives may give off the aroma of Christ. (2 Cor 2:15) (CCC 1294).

The sign of the cross

The bishop traces a cross with the chrism on the forehead of the candidate. This sign of the cross is also significant; it is the seal or mark of Christ himself. The gift of the Spirit is intended precisely to unite us to Christ and make us like him. The confirmed are to bear witness by their lives to the passion and resurrection of Christ, to the paschal mystery. It also reminds us that it was the Crucified One, still marked by his wounds, who breathed the Spirit upon his disciples (*Jn* 20:19ff). The Christian upon whom this sign has been set is marked with his owner's brand, signifying his membership of Christ's flock and the promise of divine protection.[12] Finally, for the Fathers, the signing with the cross also possessed great eschatological importance as the token by which the faithful are to be recognised in the hereafter. Normally in the early Church, the "signing" was the last ceremony of a candidate's initiation.

Be sealed with the Gift of the Holy Spirit

It is never a gesture alone, nor some material thing, which constitutes a Christian sacrament, but always a gesture - washing, anointing, breaking bread, touching - accompanied by a *form of words* which express and define the meaning of what is happening.

---

[12] Cf. *CCC* 1296

The most important revision in the new ritual is the new sacramental *form,* that is, the words to be recited when the anointing with chrism takes place. The new sacramental words, "Be sealed with the gift of the Holy Spirit," replace "I sign you with the sign of the cross and confirm you with the chrism of salvation. In the name of the Father and of the Son and of the Holy Spirit." The latter formula, it was felt, did not express clearly enough what was being symbolised in this sacrament, namely the gift of the Holy Spirit. Pope Paul VI stated this explicitly: in the rite of Confirmation, "the faithful receive the Holy Spirit as gift." The so-called new formula is attested already in the fourth and fifth century Church and resembles the ancient formula of the Byzantine Church, by which the personal gift of the Holy Spirit on the day of Pentecost is recalled.

"The external anointing expresses an inward sealing and a spiritual anointing"

The external anointing, then, expresses an inward sealing, or signing, and a spiritual anointing. "Be sure not to regard chrism merely as ointment," warned Cyril of Jerusalem to his catechumens. "Just as the bread of the Eucharist after the invocation of the Holy Spirit is no longer just bread, but the body of Christ, so the holy chrism after the invocation is no longer ordinary ointment but Christ's grace, which through the presence of the Holy Spirit instills his divinity into us... the body is anointed with visible ointment, and the soul is sanctified by the holy, hidden Spirit." There are passages in the New Testament which speak of Christians as being sealed by the Spirit and references to spiritual anointing. "In him [Christ] you too learned to believe, and had the seal set on your faith by the promised gift of the holy Spirit" (*Eph* 1:13); "Do not distress the God's holy Spirit, whose seal you bear until the day of your redemption comes" (*Eph* 4:30); "It is God who gives both us and you our certainty in Christ; it is he who has anointed us, just as it is he who has put his seal on us, and given us a foretaste of his Spirit in our hearts" (*2 Cor* 1:21-22). The sealing then is a guarantee that the Holy Spirit will always be present; "by this anointing the confirmand receives the 'mark' or seal of the Holy Spirit" (*CCC* 1295)

The Kiss of Peace

Having sealed the candidates with chrism and marked them with the sign of the cross, the bishop embraces each of them as a brother or sister: "Peace be with you"; to which the newly confirmed replies, "And also with you." This is an extremely ancient greeting, still found in the Middle East. This is a gesture of affection, congratulations and welcome: the Church rejoices.

4. Yesterday and Today

Origins of Confirmation

Since almost all the problems concerned confirmation spring from its peculiar history, it is necessary to give some account of its practice through the ages.

From the first days of the Church as recorded in the Acts of the Apostles, the rite of baptism had been completed by the laying on of hands for the gift of the Spirit. There are two passages in the Acts of the Apostles which describe an outpouring of the Spirit as a sort of confirmation of Baptism, and these may help us to understand the sacrament of Confirmation. These two episodes describe a rite imparting a gift of the Holy Spirit which was connected with baptism yet distinct from it, involving a laying-on of hands. Once Philip the deacon had preached and conferred baptism, the Apostles sent Peter and John to the converts. On their arrival "they prayed for them, that they might receive the Holy Spirit; for as yet he had not come upon any of them, because they had only been baptised in the name of the Lord Jesus. Then they laid their hands on them and they received the Holy Spirit" (*Acts* 8:14-17). Later Paul carried out the same rite at Ephesus; "On hearing this they were baptised in the name of the Lord Jesus; and when Paul laid his hands on them, the Holy Spirit came down on them, and they began to speak in tongues and to prophesy" (*Acts* 19:5-6).

These passages indicate that after Baptism of water there was a second rite - the imposition of hands - by which the newly baptised received the Spirit. Thus the initiation begun with baptism was completed with the gift of the Holy Spirit. In these texts a distinction is made between the effects of baptism and the effect of the imposition of hands. Baptism remits sin and marks entry into the Church; the imposition of hands gives the Spirit. The Letter to the Hebrews (8:1-5) also cites a laying on of hands which is distinct from baptism.

"Baptism remits sin and marks entry into the Church; the imposition of hands gives the Spirit"

In these texts a distinction is made between the effects of baptism and the effect of the imposition of hands. In Acts, Baptism of water is above all for the forgiveness of sin; the imposition of hands relates to the gift of the Holy Spirit. But the two are intimately connected; they are two complementary aspects of entry into the Christian community. This second rite - the imposition of hands by which the newly baptised received the Spirit - was reserved to the Apostles.

In the early Church

Anointing was also introduced at an early date as a post-baptismal rite. The very early Christian liturgies of initiation included a post-baptismal laying on of hands, as well as a rite of anointing, but it is not always clear whether this was a sacrament separate from Baptism. Even today in the current rite of Baptism of children, there is an anointing with chrism after baptism, foreshadowing the later confirmation of the child. However, the existence of a second rite distinct from baptism is clearly attested from the 3rd century onwards. Around the year 200, Tertullian speaks of a post-baptismal anointing and the imposition of hands that called down the Holy Spirit upon the baptised, in a passage which lists all the rites of initiation:

> The flesh is washed, that the soul may be cleaned; the flesh is anointed, that the soul may be consecrated: the flesh is signed that the soul may be fortified;
> flesh is shaded by the imposition of the hand, so that the soul may be illumined by the Spirit; the flesh is fed on the body and blood of Christ that the soul may be feasted on God.

A few years later in Rome the *Apostolic Tradition* of Hippolytus lays down that the newly baptised, upon emerging from the waters are to be anointed by a priest, and then, after dressing, led to the bishop. The bishop is to pray over them with outstretched hand, asking God, "Make them worthy to be filled with the Holy Spirit that they may serve thee according to thy will." He then pours consecrated oil upon the head and signs the forehead saying, "I anoint thee with holy oil in God the Father Almighty and Christ Jesus and the Holy Spirit." These early texts in which confirmation can be identified are very similar to what occurs today.

At this stage, it should be remembered, the rites of initiation, while developing in the direction of greater complexity, were still administered in the course of a single ceremony, the paschal vigil. Different parts of the rite gave expression to different aspects of being a Christian, but there was no question at this period of asking at which stage of the rite a person became a Christian or received the Spirit. The entire liturgy brought forgiveness of sins, and the gift of the Spirit, and united the believer to Christ, with all that that implies. The whole process signified and brought about the transformation of the person into a Spirit-filled member of Christ in the Church.

The Break-up of Christian Initiation

Originally, as we've seen, Baptism, Confirmation and the Eucharist were given in that order at one celebration, to both infants and adults. This seems to have remained the practice of the whole church until around the year 1100.

This practice manifested the unity of the rite of Christian initiation most clearly. As Christians became more numerous, and dioceses bigger, and with the almost universal practice of infant baptism from the sixth century, it became impossible for the bishop to be present at all the baptisms. East and West solved the problem in different ways. In the East the primitive unity of the three sacraments was kept by allowing priests to administer confirmation, although the oil always had to be previously blessed by the bishop. This is still the Eastern practice; communion is still given to infants after their baptism and confirmation.

While the East kept the clear link between baptism and confirmation but lost the visible involvement of the bishop, the West lost the clear link between baptism and confirmation but maintained the importance of the bishop as successor of the apostles who received the Spirit at Pentecost. This insistence on the role of the bishop led to an increasing separation of confirmation and baptism from the sixth century onwards. Nevertheless up to the twelfth century the three sacraments of initiation were given together whenever a bishop was available; and even where confirmation was delayed, the sacraments were still received in that order.

The sacraments of initiation are:

1) Baptism; 2) Confirmation; 3) Eucharist.

The Forgotten Sacrament

Events were not always favourable, however, to the development of confirmation as an independent rite. Bishops had to be willing and able to spend much time travelling round their extensive dioceses. St Bede reports that St Cuthbert toured the countryside "so that he might preach and lay his hands on those recently baptised so that they might receive the Holy Spirit." In the Penitential of Theodore of Canterbury we find the statement: A bishop may confirm in a field if it is necessary. The biographer of St Hugh of Lincoln (d. 1200) sees it as a mark of exceptional virtue that the prelate dismounted from his horse to confer the sacrament. Not only were parents slow to appreciate the importance of the rite, but the bishops themselves were often negligent in making their rounds to complete baptismal initiation by the laying on of hands. Many people went without confirmation or were delayed until a much later age. The subject of confirmation is mentioned in so many synods' decrees that it seems to have been neglected for many centuries. In the 12th century St Bernard relates that his friend St Malachy re-introduced into Ireland "the most wholesome usage of confession, the sacrament of confirmation and the contract of marriage , all of which were either unknown or neglected."

Consequently, while it was still supposed that a baptised child should ideally be confirmed as soon as possible after baptism, in practice the tendency was for the two parts of Christian initiation to drift further and further apart, and even for the second part, confirmation, to be dropped altogether. Age limits came to be set beyond which confirmation should not be deferred. In England, a council of Worcester in 1240 and another at Chichester in the following year decreed that confirmation take place within a year of baptism, but around 1280 a synod of Durham recommended the age of seven, while one at Exeter (1287) suggested three. In a council held at Lambeth in 1281, the "damnable negligence" whereby people grew old and died without being confirmed was condemned. The measure went on to forbid Holy Communion to be given to anyone not confirmed, except in danger of death, unless the person had been prevented from being confirmed by some reasonable cause.

Age of Confirmation and Order of the Sacraments

With the understanding of the sacrament as being the gift of the Spirit for the arming and strengthening of the Christian in the world, it appeared increasingly proper to defer confirmation until a child clearly seemed to need such assistance. The Catechism of the Council of Trent issued and firmly established the practice of not giving confirmation before the age of seven, referred to as the age of reason, but not later than twelve: "for confirmation has not been instituted as necessary for salvation, but that by virtue thereof we might be found well-armed and prepared when called upon to fight for the faith of Christ; and for this kind of conflict assuredly no one will consider children, who still want the age of reason, to be qualified". All the same it remained the practice everywhere for centuries to give confirmation before communion.

It was not until after the French Revolution, especially about the middle of the nineteenth century, that the custom grew up of leaving confirmation until after first communion.[13] It arose in France, then spread to Belgium and on to Austro-Hungary. Pope Pius X's desire to promote wider reception of the Eucharist led to his decree in 1905 encouraging daily Communion, followed by a decree on children's communion (*Quam singulari*) in 1910. He reduced the age of First Communion from between 12-14 years of age to the age of discretion, around seven. This was a reaction to the rigourism which had insisted on long preparation for the sacrament, but it gave the reversal of the order between confirmation and communion a firm hold, though neither he nor subsequent legislation suggested postponement of confirmation to a later age.[14] Nevertheless, this has become so much the accepted usage that some people

[13] St Therese of Lisieux gives us an interesting example of this in her autobiography: "Soon after my first Communion I went into retreat again for Confirmation, and I prepared myself with great care for the coming of the Holy Spirit; I can't understand how anyone could do otherwise before receiving this Sacrament of Love."

[14] See Aidan Kavanagh, op cit., pp. 97-101 for much more on this point.

have the idea that it is wrong for a child to be confirmed before its first communion even when this is feasible.

The modern tendency is to rediscover the normal order (Baptism-Confirmation-Eucharist). Because of the essential unity of the sacraments of initiation, it is now the policy of the Church that whenever adults, or children who have reached the age of discretion, come to the church for baptism, they will normally be baptised, confirmed and make their first holy communion in a single liturgy.[15] The Rite of Christian Initiation of Adults (1972) states:

> In accord with the ancient practice followed in the Roman liturgy, adults are not to be baptised without receiving confirmation immediately afterward, unless some serious reason stands in the way. The conjunction of the two celebrations signifies the unity of the paschal mystery, the close link between the mission of the Son and the outpouring of the holy Spirit, and the connection between the two sacraments through which the Son and the Holy Spirit come with the Father to those who are baptised

No explicit provision in this sense is made for children baptised in infancy, yet numerous texts suggest that where possible the order of the sacraments should be

[15] Rite of Confirmation, 11; cf. *CCC* 1233.

respected.[16] Thus the Catechism reads: "In the eastern rites the Christian initiation of children also begins with Baptism followed by Confirmation and the Eucharist, while in the Roman rite it is followed by years of catechesis before being completed later by Confirmation and the Eucharist, the summit of their Christian initiation" (1233). This text implies that where the rites differ with regard to *age* of reception, they need not differ with regard to order, i.e. Confirmation before Eucharist.

The separation of Confirmation from Baptism (and the Eucharist) and the subsequent association of confirmation with adolescence has led to disputes about the age of Confirmation for those baptised in infancy. There are two views on the age of Confirmation. Those in favour of a later age for Confirmation find an argument in the insistence on the need for instruction before Confirmation. A later age allows for a fuller personal participation in the sacrament. The delay, it is felt, enables the child to affirm personally all the beliefs and values he has received. It is desirable that there be some consecration to the apostolate, which is not really pertinent to babies, and a sanctification of the transition to maturity and adult life. On the other hand, it is argued that attainment of maturity is a highly individualised

[16] Constitution on the Liturgy (*Sacrosanctum Concilium*), 64-71; Rite of Christian Initiation for Adults, 34; Pope Paul VI, *Divinae consortium naturae* (1971); Rite of Confirmation, 11; Code of Canon Law 842:2; 897.

phenomena. More deeply, it is maintained that this would turn the sacrament "into some form of puberty rite"[17] Confirmation is not, and never has been, a sacrament of the personal spiritual struggle of adolescence. All this, it is felt, limits the scope of the sacrament, which is the completion of baptism, the sacrament of the mystery of Pentecost, the sacrament of the Holy Spirit and the sacrament that prepares Christians for the Eucharist. From this point of view there is no objection to giving the sacraments to infants and young children, for they will have within themselves the principle enabling them to act as witnesses of Christ when they develop.

In the new rite no new ruling is made as to the age at which those baptised in infancy should receive the sacrament. In accordance with the custom of the Western Church this is generally to be deferred to the age of seven, but each Episcopal conference is allowed to decide for a later age.

St Thomas, in a text quoted by the Catechism, gives a warning not to approach the age of confirmation in too rigid a way "Age of body does not determine age of soul. Even in childhood man can attain spiritual maturity" (1308). Young children may well have to struggle against the enemies of the faith, and in a secular world, they may

---

[17] Austin Milner, OP, *Theology of Confirmation,* (Cork:Mercier Press, 1971),104.

be called to bear witness to their faith. We can think here of St Agnes, St Agatha, and the young Ugandan martyrs.

Our Lady and Confirmation

Our Lady received the Spirit at the Incarnation in her whole being, which made her become the archetype of the Church - and of Confirmation, for in that sacrament every member of the Church receives this Spirit. Indeed, Our Lady was present at all three stages that form the Christian mystery and the mystery of the Church: the Incarnation, the paschal mystery and Pentecost. She has therefore a unique relationship to the sacraments of Christian initiation. The person of the Redeemer, God and man, was formed in her womb; she was present at the foot of the cross when He worked our redemption by destroying sin and renewing life; and she was present at Pentecost when the Holy Spirit was poured out on the Church to make Christ's redemptive work operative. If Confirmation is the personal Pentecost of each Christian, then Mary is at the heart of this sacrament as she was present at the moment of Pentecost; and after Pentecost by her prayerful presence in the Christian community.

Following Our Lady in each of these events will help us to live Christ's mystery and the grace of each sacrament. During the years of the hidden life, she was "hid with Christ in God." At the foot if the Cross she shared in Christ's self-emptying "in what is perhaps the deepest kenosis of faith in human history".[18] From Pentecost she accompanies the present work of salvation in Christ, accompanying the Church's journey through time. Mary is found at every stage of the spiritual life.

At the Cross Our Lady appeared as mother of the Church; at Pentecost, she appeared as the "godmother of the Church - a strong and sage godmother... When an adult is being baptised the godmother helps with the preparations and this was what Mary did with the apostles and does with us."[19]

In all this, as in so much else, Mary is our companion and model. Let us ask her who was full of the Holy Spirit to nurture and foster the growth of Christ's life in us, so that we can say that we not only belong to Christ but that we have become Christ.

---

[18] John Paul II, *Redemptoris Mater*, p. 37

[19] R. Cantalamessa, *Mary, Mirror of the Church* (Collegeville: Liturgical Press, 1992), p. 145.

FURTHER READING

On the Sacraments:

Baptism (CTS Publications, 2004; Do 712).
Confirmation (CTS Publications, 2004; Do 713).
Eucharist (CTS Publications, 2004; Do 714).
Reconciliation (CTS Publications, 2004; Do 716).
Anointing (CTS Publications, 2004; Do 711).
Marriage (CTS Publications, 2004; Do 710).
Holy Orders (CTS Publications, 2004; Do 715).

Finn, Thomas M, *Early Christian Baptism and the Catechumenate: Italy, North Africa and Egypt* (Liturgical Press, 1992)

Finn, Thomas M, *Early Christian Baptism and the Catechumenate: West and East Syria* (Liturgical Press, 1992)

Kavanagh, Aidan OSB, *Confirmation: Origins and Reform* (New York: Pueblo, 1988)

Kavanagh, Aidan OSB *The Shape of Baptism: The Rite of Christian Initiation* (Pueblo, 1978)

Milner, Austin, OP, *Theology of Confirmation* (Cork, 1972)